House Is an Enigma

EMMA BOLDEN

House Is an Enigma

EMMA BOLDEN

SOUTHEAST MISSOURI STATE UNIVERSITY PRESS
2018

National
Endowment
for the Arts
arts.gov

House Is an Enigma
By Emma Bolden

Copyright 2018 Emma Bolden

ISBN: 978-0-9979262-8-6
Softcover: $15.00

First published in 2018 by
Southeast Missouri State University Press
One University Plaza, MS 2650
Cape Girardeau, MO 63701
www.semopress.com

Cover Art: "The Company of Wolves" by Sidsel Sørensen
Cover Design: James Brubaker

Library of Congress Cataloging-in-Publication Data

Names: Bolden, Emma, author.
Title: House Is an enigma / by Emma Bolden.
Description: Cape Giradeau : Southeast Missouri State University
    Press, 2018.
Identifiers: LCCN 2018009029 | ISBN 9780997926286
Classification: LCC PS3602.O652 A6 2018 | DDC 811/.6--dc23
LC record available at https://lccn.loc.gov/2018009029

Table of Contents

For my parents, who taught me that even if it seems like you have nothing, if you have love, you have everything.

Thank you for giving me everything and more.

I remember a house where all were good...

— Gerard Manley Hopkins,

"In the Valley of the Elwy"

These are the foundations of our mourning.

—Michel de Montaigne

I

An Unmothered Guide to Grief

First, wax your fingers. Fill the cup of your mouth with raw
egg, your ears with cotton culled straight from its stalk,
for someone will say that grief is seven stages you must

play through in costume, and someone will say that grief is
a beauty because it means you have lost, because it means you
have loved. Understand: grief steps heavy in the valleys

beyond have, beyond hold, in the spaces where there are no
objects nor arms. Like any loved thing, your little grief deserves
to be nurtured. Let it lie down in skied pastures, speaking

the green taste off grass tongues. Carve a door inside of
your door. Carve a door inside of your belly, draw an arrow
with blackberry jam. Point to the place meant to grow

a sweetness you could love inside of its weepings, its sleep-
less shit and storms, the syncopated terror of its song. Let grief
be your most favorite. Let grief be the song that troubles down

the keys of your spine, out the flat bass of your feet
and into the room standing open as a safe that ate its own
key. Do not be afraid. Let loss become your best, the one

sweet spoon of a friend who is always walking towards
because she knows no other way out of away.

Creation Myth with Language and Angels

In the shape of a flood rained down
the ranked angels, one by dove by done, &
the lip of the shore & the lip of the sea

gathered their wishes (which grew shells &
armored) gathered their fishes (which refused
to be men). Later, men made names

for their causes (sin, law, silence) to make
effect less abhorrent, more deserved. Later,
women learned that beauty is loss & love

the fear that the beloved will become
too beautiful to keep. This is the time before
language meant run. This is the time

before electricity meant somewhere
a language waits for a mouth. This is
the time before the word never

meant your mouth is a place to store
teeth & their hungers, where feather melts
into an alleluia (which, along with god,

is the first word we learned
to use for our fear).

Pain Serves

                         every human understanding. We all hate. We would
do anything. We are as inevitable as death. Some of us believe
in necessity, which is another word for God. Life is where we live without

happy or hopefully. We endure our answers daily. Here a woman
wears tears and hoop earrings. Here a woman wears red & wields a chair.
Each of us are differently engulfed (here a woman wears a white

dress & wields a knife) by a long list of abstractions. Here a woman
wears invisible skin. Here we see inside of her body, the lines
that will never become a map.

Because the Body Is a Place Strange Unmapped

I walked the rented city, the swath of sod
beside the creek. I walked the landscape I knew

as land until I knew it & its cold as intimately
as oxygen, the banks beaded with so many eyes

I couldn't understand seeing. When the first
feathers first needled through my arms I mistook

their beginnings for a rash. I lotioned & long-sleeved
each arm they pricked by calamus, by rachis, the smooth

wash of vane. By these means I became. By this I mean
I was naked & not naked, the way the animals are

naked & not naked, the way they are in their bodies
& not in their bodies, their faces stuffed with teeth above

the delicately wired trap of a jaw. I thought I'd learn flight
but I just found feather, the secrecy of dark & star & beast.

The First Time After Surgery

He wanted to see the scar. Of course
there was a night before: satay
and sake, cigarettes and Moscato.
Enough clichés to move my hand

to the light switch, my lips
to explain why I needed the dark.
And then kiss the dark parts
of him. In the next day's light

he thumbed down the waist
of my jeans, then the length
of the scar over what had been
my body, split. A window. Outside,

the pear tree bragged about the flowers
in its hands. He said I was beautiful.
It did not change me, or anything.

I Am Writing a Story and You Are Reading It

There are no ways left to pretend. Thank you for suspending
your disbelief like a bridge. It can carry much weight:
a thousand pounds of mustard seed, loaves and loves
dividing endlessly over the colors of fish turning their lights

on and off for the sea. You expect me to believe in language.
You expect an image and an ending, but love has never been
perfect or promising. This is the story of crimson. It's a bull
in the crowd's mouth. It's a cape that might as well be a rose.

Excavation, Exhibition

Of the year we wore leather & guitar music sweet with distortion
I remember the taste of peppermint bright as teeth, as the lime
balanced on gin's balcony. When the train trestle tired of its own
gravity, it unglassed every window until I couldn't sing or

break or sleep, I couldn't stop locked doors, blood, recognition,
pallor & the lofi buzz of forever translated into the language
of that radio, that same damn Aerosmith song. I was in love &
everything mattered & meant that I missed a man, displayed on

lawns & car hoods & parking lots, gassed & stationed. I saw
him in the same way I saw the museum. Displayed inside glass:
a man who lived to be dead. For five thousand years snow was
gentlesweet, preserving him as skin & tufts of once-was-hair.

The self I couldn't love looked & head-shaking said *doesn't he look
like last night's chicken*, & all through ancient Greece & by the Rosetta
Stone, under the marble men who'd lost their arms but kept
their laurel leaves & penises, I couldn't stop thinking, why would

he & I & time & light never be a beauty or jewel-lasting of a thing.
I could've lived for one forever & another forever glassed inside hope,
which is always a lie, gentlesweet, preserving. I could've lived framed
in the grays of the photograph he took after he'd refused to light

my cigarette. He centered me in the cross-hair of his lens, he said *never
start & then you'll never have to stop* & I thought if I believed enough
that could mean I love you.

It was no more predictable

than a lunch or a death
it wasn't September or the house before windows
opened   wouldn't I know if we all had grown
gossamer   there is too much wool on his tongue
& after the sherbets & armagnac   & he was standing
by that evergreen in the center of France   & that
was the one time & everything   looking   & so we
decided not to decide   god was not happy   god
was at the same time never & always & any way
god was never a part of this plan & I said in your
hands of course there's a sweetness   of course it was
the last thing I meant   when we lay & let the night
give us back our clothing   I was thinking of his
mouth & its fullness   its stars in their distance & in
their thousands & we would never be anything
more or less than light

Let's Talk About the Weather, That's Probably for the Best

I remembered. I'd listened to the rain. And then the sound returned to
me. Many nights I lost my sleep. Once I found it by putting my body
in a chair. Once I folded myself in my clothes neatly in the bedroom's
corner. Once I awoke on the bathroom floor. I was a child, so there
were rules. There were places where my arms could make an X. There
were places that belonged to me only. There were places that belonged
to me that still were not mine to touch. So how can I make words for
what her hands did. How can I make words for. This is the circle from
which I won't step. My right foot may leave, but what's left will never
know why. Once I awoke in the hallway beneath that built-in desk.
There were the sounds of weather. A virgule of a girl in an orange
coat and all of the words her hands said and unsaid. This I remember.
So I could make the word *take*, which means what it means when it
leaves behind *give*. Here is the line I'll leave blank instead of speaking.
Instead of all of this, all of this weather and rain.

Melancholy Inside the Body

So many umbrellas have I
collected & no number ever
enough. They turn themselves

upside down & still
can't hold all of the rain
& its expectant sadnesses.

I take my body walking past
a house & inside its bricks
my neighbor is singing. She

& my body & I don't know
the words. There are too many
sunsets. Every watch is lost. I am

my own globe made of only
seas & I'm spinning. Did I mean
tears or tears? Somewhere every

sock I've lost is hiding. Every
girl & every boy I've lost,
hiding. I'm not crying. On my palm

the lines gather into a sailboat.
It's waiting & the wind is high.
Did I ever mean to say shore?

Like a Trick Belonging to the Eye or the Mind

Down the small river that started at one end
of what I could see & stopped at the other I had

a glimpse of an it floating & white. A newspaper.
Or a swan. I said I'm sorry while my sky stuffed itself

until it was too full of ducks & their sounds & it had
to become quiet. So it became night. I was quiet.

I didn't say or anything & watched as around me every
emptiness became its own wall. It was the game I liked

to play because it was the game God liked to play
with me, with every being who travels too far & into alone.

House Is an Enigma

House is not a metaphor. House has nothing
to do with beak or wing. House is not two

hands held up and angled towards each other. House
is not its roof or the pine straw on its roof. At night,

its windows and doors look nothing like a face.
Its stairs are not vertebrae. Its walls may be

white, but they are not pale skin. House does not
appreciate your pun on its panes as pains.

House does not appreciate because house
does not have feelings. House has no aesthetic

program. House does what it does, which is
not doing. House does not sit on its foundations.

House *exists* in its foundations, and when the wind
pushes itself to full gale, house is never the one crying.

The Study of Surfaces, the Study of Curves

Here in this room I am mapping this room. I am making it flat so it will fit on paper. I use shades of blue as a translation of space. On a map all griefs are standard, as are all desires, and a curve is only one of many reasons why a mountain is a mountain. A line is a notation of all forces and magnitudes. For instance: *I am a series of dots.* For instance: *you are a thick backslash.* A failure of language. Here in this room I am finding this room is more useful than language or failure. Here there are walls wearing paint and light, and each is a plane meeting another plane at all of the right angles. If you continue to seek definitions, there will be only temperatures. I am trying to tell you. There will be only rising. Nothing will be or will have its inverse. Here I am in this room, and here in this room, that will always be true.

Alma

I can say a soul stood inside of me the same
way I say bricks stand on bricks to be walls. I
can say there was emptiness, glass, the window

that was the body. Through it my soul and I watched
the trees being trees. They carried their colors. They

changed and changed. Sunday was a room where we
learned about God, who was a tongue that turned
shrubs to ashes. God was a lamb flying white

winged as a pigeon. God could see no difference
between dove and pigeon, hands and wings,

every feather lost and hollowed as every word. And if
you could let him in you were holy. Alma, my sweet
soul, we knew what we knew. Then how did we sin?

Yes, I Would Like to Imagine the Self

as a bird or a plane far
from our abhorrent geometries. No

one has a box shaped like
a heart, a tambourine, a set

of bass notes properly equipped
for amplification. Together

we are still a you and an I,
a saint and a landscape

in miniature, a diorama
of dime-store bulls, of feathers

plucked from their birds
like the last note sung

by a hot mic inside of
a hot gymnasium. No.

When I see the sun I feel
no emotion as real as

anything chemical, as if
inside this skyline there is

no synonym for night.

Of Blue Morning

The egg cracked into itself and its shell.
There were secrets and nobody knew.

She was sure. She was sure there was
nothing to be done or doing. She took

her antidepressants with coffee. She told
the blinds to open with a twist of her hand.

In the room sat a television, vacant as bravery.
There was something she needed to understand.

She was sure. Around her sat air and electricity.
Every slick from a tire and a road gave a warning.

She didn't mean to or not to. Even the ceiling
above her curved with another question.

Hysterectomy/Recovery

Though I didn't know how to begin or believe, I held in
myself expectation. Awareness. A palpable fit. Every garden

a window through which I petalled off hopes. There was nothing

so alarming as a sky. Who knew if an elegance walked invisible
beside me or on stolen feet. Or if all elegance is the act of being

invisible after all. If after all the spirit is indivisible from the body.

Or a glamor slit from this spilt sack of skin. I have never had
nor been enough. Every sundress is an ache. What a pink

unpleasantness, the idea of touch. An earth let loose and loss

the only record of its revolutions, its unguarded roots. A sky
rinsing from itself the pointless trash of spring.

I Was Told Not to Write About the Body

I was told not to give the body
a name so I let it walk aimless &
alien. I was told not to think

of the body & so I made the body
into a night. I was told to be more
positive. I was told that I was always

the one in charge of uplifting
my own self & so I uplifted my
skirts until I could see my body

walking both into & out of a night.
I was told I would be charged. I was
told to see the body as light so I made it

a sky. I gave it a sack full of stars.
I slept in its lacks. I asked it to be,
asked it to stay, asked God

in every name I knew to let my body
& me be. I was not an answer. I was not
an answer. I was told I shouldn't write

about the body or the deaths
that grayly hung by claw & upside
down inside & so I made the body

a clearing & the deer who stood
inside. I made the body a deer's mouth.
I tasted the leaf greenly chewed inside,

I felt the velvet of its nose & ears &
cheeks & I felt the cold intrusion
of bullet, the raw shock & silence

of the rifle, of the stop, of the story
I was not supposed to give to the body
I was not supposed to name.

Melancholy Inside Gardens

This sadness doesn't curl inside the fact
that the blossoms will die so much
as the fact that they have blossomed, and here,

in spring honey-hot, sifting pollen into
the opened bowls of such yellows. Into
the center where sweetness is held

they gather a landscape of blurs. This sadness
isn't what we're allowed, which is to see
in glimpses only, but that we are allowed to see

any of an all. The hummingbird thrum
of wing. Sun and its punishments of light. Sky
and its freezing, impenetrable as blue.

II

That Cold Snap, April's Last

The weather was an ice cube against her
bared pink hand. Wool skirts and knee
socks, the sound of wood giving up its ash.
An umbrella blown backwards to show itself

in metal bones and joints. The weather was wind
sharp as peppermint. It was hair burl-curled and
uncombable. It left its red marks in her eyes
and her cheeks. From inside the house, the weather

was a song heard from a neighbor's distance, all
woodwinds and violins, a voice rushing through
the high notes. She was thinking of ice pops in plastic,
the kind that sliced her mouth at its corners, the insides

of her cheeks. The weather was the kind of lie she told
when she said that she was fine. The weather was an
envelope and she was sealed inside. She took off her jacket
so it could sit in the passenger seat. She wanted to know

what cold meant. She wanted to know what meaning
meant. She parked the car. The weather sat above
the pavement and shimmered until she thought
she saw, far as a distance, what should have been a ghost.

My little apparition, my little ghost

                           & from under
the wave was what?   I remember words & surface
& I remember that   time   was a place. I can't
say. There was rain. & every branch busied itself with
its breaking. & I said what if   that lie was the best
part of me. You were inclined to agree,   we both had
chairs to sit in & that story   about the fox. We liked
to tell each other. It was easy   to think of the sky &
the stars constellated   inside of it. It was easy to
think of them as numbers, set into sets, to think of
the curved boundaries of night. You were saying. The
fox might have been   a dog, you couldn't tell,   the
chicken coop was doomed anyway, & the nests & the
eggs that jeweled them. & a zero where   there
should've been wire,   & a door that kept saying air
air   air. If I believed meaning was everywhere. If I
believed the waters themselves were air. Nothing
started or stopped & no   one held an aegis up in
angry moods. You were saying   a fox maybe or
maybe a dog & it doesn't   matter when it all comes
down to   & so I held the promise   a quail egg in
my mouth. It haunted. All of the mountains gathered
up into their clouds & every city emptied   into sea,
into fear.

Deposition: On That Night & All That Was After

The sedan pushed its high beams over the county
which was its roads & its fields & in them the animals,

who watched us with their invisible eyes. He said
do you want to just park here & I said *are you serious*

& he said *no, I'm not serious, I'm Jeremy.* We were always
going on like that. In the fields every ear of corn had its stalk

& nothing sounded like music. Did I want to take him
inside of me or did I want to know if inside of me

there was an I that was me. There was an appreciable
difference. When the temperature fell I knew no one

was a hero with a jacket anymore. He said *we might as well
be a movie* & I said *well how do you know that we aren't.* Did I

want to take or did I want to know. Inside of me there was
an I, there was a night with its mouth full of stars.

After the Beginning

There was too much to not talk about
beneath the papered globes hung lit
as the ceiling in the new Thai restaurant
in the old strip mall, a lost tooth
of a space circled in string lights, sweating off

ice & effort against the air conditioning
because August is a bastard straight from Carolina
to the Georgia coast, you said, & anyway
even if we had found between ourselves a nothing
to say it felt obscene, just saying, so we busied

ourselves with asking instead (*what kind of basil,
where to buy lemongrass?*). The waitress toothed
into her smile, blushing youngly bright &
smoothly beautiful, cultured as a laboratory
pearl & every bit as eager as we ordered another

neon round of drinks (yours spark blue, mine
violet as night terrors) (we needed to keep
our mouths full, we had reached the end of our
yessings). Our fingers flapped awkward as napkins
(in that moment I felt as if nothing anymore

had wings) & so the waitress asked the owner
about the lemongrass, came back diamond-shined
as any answer (that can sweet, sparkle, run away
from a finger just after a bride tells his windshield
her name name name). It came from the old country,

the waitress said, & you (rum-tongued, blue-warm)
said *do you mean smuggled* (it was nice enough
for a moment to joke, unpacked at the table), laughed
about customs & gym bags, jars of peanut butter
hollowed out to hold the lemongrass in an absence

inside, & so we made it to the check, through the last
dreg-drips of our third drinks & even to the moment
in which I stood under the arch of your arm, framed
by the door frame. We walked into the dark & the lights
& lines that made an empty space into a parking lot (with us

walked a freedom we both recognized, tooth-smiled,
gin-sung). In our separate cars we gave our separate
thank Gods to the roads that drove us away from our each
& our other & so we never once had to talk about the space
between me walking this week & not walking last week,

between this walking week & the next not-walking week,
between body & mobility (when will it goddamn stop me,
will it, that sick something smuggled inside of my body,
curled like a question inside spine & nerve, waiting,
waiting, a leaf ripping the roots off its very own tree).

The Reports of the Largest Moon in Ten Years

were all lies, all stories that the evening news anchored
in the sky. The moon perched against their predictions, a fat
white finch. That was the year I spent myself, falling into and out
of time and of love. We stood in our usual lawn under its usual light.

A friend handed me an axe. And blesséd be the friend
who knows me well enough to know my anger
builds itself inside my self, a castle fortressed
with a thousand verbs, all bricked synonyms

for silence. Blesséd be the tree, grayed in the gray light
that lit us, as if it had built itself for this. A friend said,
throw. I threw. I stood with all that I couldn't
see: the song the axe sang as it traveled, and the note

it left inside the tree, and above the stars—which were dead,
which were living—and the great gray bullet of a moon
shooting itself, as large as any ending, as any thought I ever
had about what is and what isn't, in all that time and space.

Melancholy in Mike Sheroda

Somebody I knew loved somebody,
I remember, & she turned every tune
inside & out & into his name, into *O*

Mikey you're so fine you're so fine you blow
my mind hey Mikey, into *muh-muh-muh-muh*
Mike Sheroda, & though I've forgotten

hers, his is the name I sing into
the inside-out empty of calendar boxes
spilling the name of the girl I knew

while holding the name of the boy
that she knew, & if I remembered
I would find her in the listings & libraries,

I would find her in numbers & letters
& into the inside-out empty of asphalt & bare
wires between us I'd say, *All day I have been*

singing, tumbling the towels I have been singing,
folding the machines I have been singing,
in washing & walking & aching I have been

singing, & can you tell me if we really did
share an ever, if there was in that ever a car
& sheet music, if there were walls that held

us up after the beer & the hamburgers, if
there really was a space in which we breathed
& trashed & laughed together & even then

were we singing, were we singing bright
lipped into & against all of this death?

House Is Writing A Symphony

House gathers the sighs of the mattress you settle
atop, the soprano complaint of each spring. With every rain,

House cues the acorn-roll of its squirrels. Listen
and you'll hear horses within House's ceiling. If you adjust

the water heater, House will switch to the sad ballad
of fan blades, the pizzicato tap of the ice tray. House has to

express itself somehow. When the day's lights dim
to a backdrop of night, House makes itself a microphone

amplifying every shudder of bedclothes, every shallow rustle.
Your toss. Your turn. And when the cries leave your throat

like animals, hoarse and roaming, House perches on the edge
of its foundations. House uses your howls as its middle C.

The Talking Cure

The therapist shows me an egg.
I fork the yolk. She shows me
an inkspill and I say *both*
halves of the brain and the fissure

between them. She stands a small
horse on her palm and I say
the blankets. They break
its hair. She brings in a clown

and I say *I'm not sure*
where you're going with this.
Then we are in a field. The therapist
points up. I say *no birds.*

She points down. I say *ditto.*
When she holds a worm between
her two top and two bottom teeth,
I say *hunger.* She says *by hunger*

you are healed. I say *you don't know*
the half of it. I mean the worm. She grins
and we sit separately in our separate nests,
where even the ink spots are hatching.

For the Doctor Who Suggested I Try to Explain How It Feels to Be Barren

I am sorry for trying not to | write I'm new | I needed |when you asked me to | doctor I am sorry | I cannot because | the breast can't | be a breast | I will never | am I complaining | my friends I am a careful | talker | I'm sorry because I cannot | I'm sorry because I knew | you meant no | harm because | I knew you | didn't know me & my | body I'm sorry because this | is the secret | to be kept | clean I was taught this | body is an obscenity | private by name | it's my | job to keep | sorry public I'm not coded | an open source | home is not the grocery | store is not the place where | you will find me | right | instead is a place I can say | that I is not where | I can take ten years | worth & theory | to prove that speaking | turns to confusion | a hole or an eye | now is not the | I say yes to every | sorry | no it's totally | I anyway | understand | this palm is not a safe | I went home to maybe | mangoes are no actuality | if we share the shared construction | peel & flesh & seed | the eye speaks | in this the poem | I can speak | only mangoes | & pits & peel | I am ashamed | I am ashamed | what about this says | body besides the fact | that it exists | what is taking | so long | it hurts in the kind | of way when peeled | down & pared & pit | by the knife | discarded this particular | naked left | behind afraid | I lost because | this is my afraid body | ashamed as hello | as the only girl trying | to say I won't | I can't

Melancholy in Definitions

Whatever love is, it isn't the thousand
points of grass raised over the field,
or the spot of sky each blade pins

at each stubborn angle. It isn't the angle
between my shoulder & its blade
or between his shoulder & his blade. It is

& it isn't a blade held against the shirt
that holds itself against his skin, his body.
There is forever an instead beyond

the place we call body. There is forever,
which is an instead made of night & its gray
way of sliding to settle the asphalt's argument

by licking a path between the pines, & there
are all of these times & trees & streets
between the angles of my body & the angles

of his body collapsed, small & green & sweet
as a blade of grass turned into a whistle
between his far & gentle teeth.

Even If You Aren't, House Is Listening

House isn't going to fall for it. House has held
you inside its rooms and seen you there naked

and with the lights on. House was unimpressed. House
trusts your resolution less than you do. House knows

that if in January you pry the pine straw from its gutters
and its grasp, by February it will all be back. The squirrels

will help. They're on House's side. House knows that he
will stay with her even when you tell yourself he's coming

or you're leaving. House has no need to tap your phone.
House is the one who holds your phone. All of its days

and its nights, House is listening. And when in the dark
you feel too tightly held and beg House and yourself

to forget, House can't. House won't. Don't think
House doesn't want to know what House knows.

Of Flora, Of Fauna

The women are beautiful but they are not
gardens, nor are the gardens beautiful

women. The clearing clears to another
clearing. The heart is a copse

of trees waving and waiting and hearing.
The heart is an ear of its own. When summer

comes with its sounds each tree will tell
its twigs: *matches*. There will be wind and all

in bloom winding within it to spark.
There will be smoke and smoke will be

signal. Every tree speaks to the heart.
Every tree tells it the way of all things.

Bark and the soft flesh underneath, burning.
Heart and the beauties it keeps, burning.

The Cities We Love Are the Ones That Are Drowning.

Once you had a dream of a boat & when
you awoke your arms wouldn't stop being

oars. I'm sorry you can't have the sea &
all of it ambient as sound, twisted to turn into

the shape of the conch while sleeping,
while waking. You were in bed & I was in bed

& then there was rain. My head lay full of
day, its throb & song, & verbs & violins

swollen to cello. The smell your hair kept &
my pillows. What was the matter

of two cups of coffee, two eggs fried &
their yolks hanging. Precisely. As the boarding

pass folding itself inside your billfold. The plane put

you inside of the air I watched. I

could hold it & the you inside of it between

my finger & my thumb. It was easy. There

was the lesson that comes with endings, that

it is best to love what you lose. Then

you won't have to keep your love (f)or

it. Forget all of the whats that I said & you can

have the sea if you want it.

49

Between Sea and Sky

If the moon is a pale horse riding
across the mute plane of night, what
then are stars but a thousand wolf eyes.

Patience. The pupil of a cat widens
to catch the light off a river like prey.
And the beach we together watched

is dreaming, under the blue dome we
together called sky it is dreaming.
Under the green beaks of waves

a thousand fish move into the mouths
of a thousand larger fish. I've forgotten
the part about waking. I've forgotten

the part about walking, which happens,
and in so many directions. Home
is a sentence that ends with

an exclamation of footprints towards
the sea and its mouth, the jagged
and pretty little waves of its teeth.

III

The gods have a bullet

that whistles your initials as it estimates the circumference
of the circle they themselves jewel-set between your eyes.
The gods chatter, gather their hems outside the nursery window.
They're waiting for the ghost inside you to be born. The gods

have plans for the room your body will be once they evict you.
They measure from your patella to your ankle, from your left
wrist to your right wrist, from the curve of the ear that your mother
lullabied to the curve of the lip your lover at first kissed, later bloodied.

To the gods, the sweet meat inside of your skull is only meat,
and only sweet enough to tempt the vulture's beak and tongue.
Once emptied, the overturned bowl of your skull will balance
itself beneath the earth, which is patience, which is a god's work,

which is knowing the worth of the body is blossom, rot, and bruise,
not the person inside who grows hungry enough to believe
she is a soul. The gods have a bullet and a beautiful temper and a love
as blank as every musk-scented secret growing thick between thigh

and mind. The gods have built a bomb that protects the dwelling
and shatters the dweller. It's called your body. It ticks. It ticks. The gods
don't mind. They are worshippers of waiting, dreaming of the roots
that will unlock the ribs caging your one and precious, ordinary heart.

Because of the House We Have Built for Our Language

Both moss and nightfall creep and crawl,
neither respectfully nor respectively. Over time,
paper leaves its spine, which lacks the durability
of bone. Bone is strung to bone with spinal cord,

which is not a sound. Tongue is both a sound and
the muscle that makes it. Skin is both the covering
and the act of uncovering. The heart is an organ
that seventy-two times per minute pumps blood

into meaning, which is not red but blue. The heart
is an organ with four chambers, which are not rooms.
Rooms are places we build for ourselves to live
inside of the belief that we were built for living.

On the Self-Guided Tour of the Fountain of Youth

The cannon fired. Over sedge & sawgrass the sound
shot out, an obscenity, & every tree revealed itself
as a gathering of branches, & every branch revealed

the motion stilled inside it, loosed by the sound. There
were shadows behind the leaves until they became birds.
That was the last time I remember my body as a verb. I ran

to the marsh & its waters, its quiet salting the shore.
Three weeks later came the morning I woke & could not walk.
I lifted each leg by the hollow behind its knee, angled each

over the side of the bed, where they stayed. I felt nothing
like a warning inside of them. A whir of wings. A wave
of reverie that would never break. A terror impossibly still.

X

A shattering silence. Then the crude language of machines.
Lying on the doctor's table, I am as flat as the table.

I am lying. The body was born to obscure, to commit
by its being the sin of omission. What blue floats inside

of us, an interior of sky as unseen as the seen. When
the doctor says *turn*, I turn. My body follows.

The doctor is a technician. His language is calm metal
coiled as tightly as the coils that thrum through their work

above myself. Into my self. When Röntgen discovered the x-ray
he saw it first as a shimmer around his wife and her body. Then

he saw inside his wife. She became her body and her body
became its own ghost, one hand a curled white cumulus

of bone lit against the grisaille of silver salts on a glass plate.
I have seen, she said, *my own death*. It gathered in the spaces

and not-spaces inside of her, then on the film that revealed
her self to herself as absence, as an ending no longer unseen.

Epithalamium

In the wick of the evening stands
a house. It settles itself on its concrete

slab & grass rushes to meet it.
Because it is a house, there are windows.

Look through one lit rectangle: first,
see the jagged teeth of stairs. Then see

a woman paused on them. She wears a yellow
dress & carries her hands, which move & move.

She has a handrail & a husband. Look
through the kitchen's windows. See his hand

testing water for warmth. See him rinse
the dishes, rinse a glass. Outside hums

with birds, with cars, & inside hums the air
conditioner, hums the kitchen faucet he uses

to rinse another glass, the bathroom faucet
she uses to rinse her hands. They on their separate

floors are humming. Their mouths & their throats
are humming. They build inside the house

a new house, made of song.

The Curse on the Ground

The mirror begins with your face floating
the surface of its silver, ends with your left

eye watching your face from the inside
of a thousand shards. A crack through which

no light gets in. There is a river and then
there is a current electric with intent. There

is the village with its children at its banks.
Then there are no banks. Even the fish

struggle, swimming their faces into each house's
locked panes of glass. There is the body breathing

and there is the body stilled, floating the surface
of silver. There are the thousand fists lifted, closed

against the line every hand carries heavy
as a story inside, telling the eye that tries

to break its own bad ending into wave and shard:
this far, this much, this held. No more.

Downburst

The day was its own warning. I was thinking of his head
on a plate in my lap. I was thinking of its soft loops of curls,

fine as the hair punched into plastic doll skulls. I felt strange
& electric & so did the sky, & when I looked out

of the window, it looked back with green. There were clouds
& clouds' low stomachs lined silver. There was a room

in which I stood alone. When the squall line quickened, the room
became aching. The room became wool. No god was there.

House Is a Mirror

House lives on top of another House, which
is House built backwards. Their feet

are their foundations. They are condemned
to touching because they were made that way.

Upside down there are no fences. Houses
are bad neighbors. One House opens its mouth

by the hinges, spits out dogs to chew the roots
of the other House's grass, which was working

towards a lawn. House is not surprised.
House is doing the same. Through weather

and wet, House opens its eyes to let light
in, let light out. House is not kind. House

sinks every purpose, wants all the walls
to slope. Sometimes when the sky puts

its rain into puddles, House sees itself and House
is sorely afraid. House will break its own roof

into shingles, House will eat itself with termite
teeth, House will rot, if that's what it takes.

The Plight Troth

Language tasted like a trick laid bare
as the back of an orchid huffing
out hothouse fumes, extravagant
as any freedom feels at first

unlike feeling, more like the numb
a doctor gives as a gift to the skin
before needling the vein

of an understanding, jelly pale,
afloat & estranged as sea. He said
he'd like to marry into innocence,
said a virgin is a value blue as a bad

joke & inside the sweet humming circle
of a she, humiliated, there quartzed
a will sharp enough to slice

any blade from grass to flame to finish
the fist that broke her like a horse
who'll never loose the wild
from her blaze of a mane.

The Coyote Doesn't Have To

believe in God or snow. She doesn't have to understand
what we mean by *dog* or *woof.* In her mothered mouth, she carries

twenty teeth, a howl, a yip, a yelp, all of the three-to-twelve pups
she birthed into sightless, soundless sleep. Half of her
litter will be skeletons before they are beasts. We may imagine

that she was warned of this. We may imagine the fear that locks
her body out of motion when she's headlocked by the brute

thrusts of her mate. She may imagine each of her pups
as a presence and an absence, as the grass and the stone
and the sky. The coyote has her reasons for running.

We have our reasons to fear her teeth. We may keep shotguns
in the garage, sheep in squares of fences. The coyote waits

for every throat, her jaw aimed just below the ear.

Shower Season

I sickened with sugar. I needed to clear the sky, stop sinking
my teeth into the corners of the ocean, into the blue

that curdles the peel of a clementine, sweet as the smile
on a news anchor's face after the cut back from a televised

disaster. Perhaps it's natural, my need to take home a meaning
not a moment, smooth & buttered, napkined over, a prison

of mints set out to celebrate two people promising to be
the same, or one person stringing together a new tune inside

the swollen cello of her body. Under the false-hooded winter
of every store's air I was conditioned to look through the pinks,

the peonied cards standing in toothed rows that grinned
greetings, belled lilies stretched over the valley of sympathy, so

I began to believe in believing, the way they told me to life. Silked
& unsuffered. I necked the tender loop of a narrative's noose.

In Every Tale About Hunger

In winter the husband walks ever northward.
The wife stays dark and light in their house,
canning the last of last summer's fruits: sad

apples that only half-made themselves,
blackberries that pricked her with their ticking

vines. He slices the soles off his shoes
to give his feet the gift of ice, a slow burn to numb.
Above him, geese gather like a bad hem. They urge

him: northward, north. He sits for a spell cast
by a lake that magicked itself into ice

while fish move their mouths and their bodies
below. When he has a vision of home, he has
a vision of walls. When she has a vision of home,

she builds another wall. She sews another dress
over her dress, then another. Another, until she knows

every wall as an answer. The horizon answers
every question he asks with blue, and then
more blue. He wants to walk to an end.

She holds the needle in her mouth. She sews a dress
into her skin, a veil over her face. His legs give up

walking. He falls into snow, that white witch
who is always wet, always a woman who wants.
When his wife has worked enough, she sews herself

into standing even while she sleeps. It's the way
she has of making. It's the way she makes to wait.

Tropes

I write about his eyes. I use specifics.
I use the following metaphors: fish, jellyfish,

jelly jars, the shove and clutch of earth
moving its magma. I don't get it

right. I read about magma. I learn
by its terms: from the Greek μάγμα, or paste;

both crystal and gas; seven hundred Celsius
to thirteen hundred Celsius. I write again. I don't

get it right. As always, I cut off my hands.
Then there's one hand left and no hand

to hold. There's always a blade. There's always
a horizon, which is sometimes the color of a sky,

sometimes the color of a blade. Words will always
be air, so I write that: *words will always be*

air. Each image asks two questions. I say they are
unaskable, so I say: *Do you love me. Are you this afraid.*

That Night in (the Car & the Inside & Outside & So)

If I call the trees spires they will still not be spires. Not even
if you should agree. Yes you. Anyway what need would a bird
have for pews. I thumbed a cross against each egg & watched

the mother wing away. When I was a child it was all in my hands.
My palms walled the church in & my fingers prayed & inside
there were people with heads & they bowed. You said *do I turn*

here & *left or right*. I said *yes* from inside of the L my left hand made.
I never remember how to remember what's right. The windshield
wouldn't stop showing off its blurred trees, the sky was a window

with a set of eyes & on each & every side there was a God someone
should belong to. That was the night my hands refused gloves, choosing
the way cold touched them, how it tended to each finger, eager as any burn.

I Was a Bad Child & I Was a Match

& then the brute interruption of spirit.
Desire & fire licked the walls clean.

There were words & they kept offering
themselves. There were, of course, ways to say.

I told myself to feel & then I felt a little like
feeling. I had stowed myself so carefully far

in some compartment hinged of muscle, doored
of bone. I knew all beginnings were subtle.

The choice I made was not a choice. I told myself
any beauty is home. The convex blush

of impatiens. Stole, mink, and fur. Hair
ribbon & velvet, sherbet, lace, I

told myself any end is a beauty. I told
myself. There's world & word in ash.

IV

Under Threat of Eden

Inside the garden I could pretend
I had caught fever, a frenzy of fire

flowers, the ochre ache one expects
of a tree. I could hear passion, a hum

trapped in the tooth of the wolf
I watched until she trusted me

with her hunger. I wore her
hide. I was a revival, an August,

a shattered crescendo of wishing
for wanting, this ragged waiting

inside of. I choked. The blood
I expected. I said that I wanted

to be flayed and carnal, to be thrust
and shuddered under any him willing

to be violent as a god. I wanted to
understand the point and the hilt

of the sword, I wanted to know
life gorged and garnet as

the howl inside of every red.
I tasted fang and honey heavy

as hatred, I tasted tongue, I wanted
this ragged with waiting, with shame.

Describe the Situation in Specific Detail

Merlot. Whiskey and vodka. Very little tonic. Sometimes seltzer. I
believed he did not break the glass on purpose. Sake, cold and hot.
The small wooden boxes he used to hold a flood. Octopus: just-dead,
light-wet. How long did I stay in the parking lot, calling the stray bones
of a cat? He said minutes, fifteen. He always guessed in increments of
five. In the morning his apartment smelled of ash and fish bones. And
in the blind light I reached for my sweater, my purse, black knit and
black leather, respectively. I believed him when he said the bird already
was dead. His questions: *you like it* and *I know you're sure* and *I know
you're ready inside.* My answers: *no* and *yes* and *no,* respectively. And the
prawn curling itself undersea of saffron broth. That ever he could stand
and stay in a scene as green as all that. I hated his riding coat. I believed
and I loved him, like hands circling my throat.

Morphine

All night the jungle scrolled by.
Its sheaths of green. Its vine-snaked

trees. Its air closed hot & dark,
the inside of a mouth. The dream

said I was I & you were you & a pair
of lips slit by speech. Every word

a tooth. I saw them, short white arrows.
I was telling you something & you

were telling me back & between
your lips the sound rolled into & over

color, magenta, azure, the vile shock
of orange. I felt disaster. The only

thing that was clear was everything,
which had its own space & sounds.

The clear arpeggios so composed with
their pain. The way sound sequenced

its ache in the spine. The way each bone
was both bell & its ringing. Nothing

was answered or obvious. Nothing so
predictable as an alarm. When I woke,

I woke with it, all the black balled inside.
My silence is my mouth.

Viscera

Believe me when I tell you: I walked
to the barn voluntarily. Let no one say
I was led. Nor was I asked to remove
my shoes, place them sole-down

in the order they kept on my feet. No
one said *stand* & I stood on the stool.
Above me the chain looped & loped
down & I saw it as beautiful. I did not

hesitate. It fit my neck & was perfect.
It was as if I had always been waiting.
Beside me hung my brother the sheep.
He was quiet. Flies sequined the hollow

half-bell of his body. His eyes were facts,
open zeroes of surprise or delight. I didn't kick
the stool away. I wanted to know the butcher.
I wanted to know his hook. My throat

felt white, felt electric, felt neither heat
nor cold. I became busy with the facts
of being & becoming not & I at very last felt
real. There was no stomach speaking hunger.

No lungs or womb to say *fill*. Had I a throat
& a mouth, had I for this stillness a tongue, I
would have thanked the hook for giving
me such forgiving, for making I not eye.

We Decided to Stop Believing in God.

Kelsey put her faith in surround sound, John
in the black skin that gummed his dog's teeth.
I wanted a challenge so I believed in mathematics.
There was an eloquence in its functions, implicit
& explicit. I admired each equation for being

gorgeous & exacting: *sub x for twelve. Carry*
the one. One to the nth power. A negative i. In six
months I'd turned fraction to decimal, *y* to thirty-six.
Even had God in one swoop of a hand shown me
the sweep of existence as a vista, even had God kept

the skywriters writing his name + my name in clouds
for three years, even had God shown up at the storm
door carrying carnations & a bag of green apples
to say *Well, I'm sorry*, it wouldn't be enough. & anyway
God kept hand & mouth shut, which was after all the point.

The Summer I Wondered Why Dresses Exist

There were always colors. He wore his war
wound secret as a kindness, as a jewel

that I could never define. Perhaps peridot.
Perhaps the way a diamond feels against

a mirror. The way a pearl feels against
two teeth. The way two teeth feel

to the ear between them. There were two
sentences I kept confusing: *I fall away from*

you/*I finally found a you.* There were such beautiful
excuses. I could identify as jewelry wrought

by love's harshest geometry, a chain on which
one hangs the lock that hides itself as a key.

House Is the Word My Doctors Used for My Body

My doctors couldn't make themselves tell me
that I couldn't have children until they made me

into a metaphor, into a house happy in the kind of story
they'd tell their own children. And in the story I became,

the House I was cried. I was the House who felt her façade hot
and snotted and wet. House had forgotten her Kleenex.

And House and I stay the space that didn't become a place.
House is not a synonym for nest. House is not an antonym

for full. House is a part without speech. House is nobody's
property. House is the emptiness that can't be addressed

in any way that feels like a home. House does not want
to talk about it. *I'm as big as a house*, House's pregnant friend

says. House's mouth makes itself smile, makes itself into
the door that I will never open, I will never close.

After Auden

The clocks aren't enough. Stop also
the feather from crowning the hoopoe's
head. Stop the beak from scissoring worm
into worm, bee into peace. Stop also
the bee. Let its wings lie slack with lack

of motion. May there be no motion. May
there be no metaphor. May the ocean lay
its long hair in the lap of shore and stay
there. And quiet. Quiet the moon. Take
from it its incessant instructions. Take

from the sky its false light in the first place.
Let us learn light as a structure built from reflection,
dark as one possible explanation. As what.
As where. As a list of sounds a mother
may use to soothe her child, her sleep.

Having lived beyond

beauty   as   a   possibility
having lived past touch past body as potential having
swum to the horizon & found it's never   anything
after   all but a line   having walked the long garden in
rainfall   in leaf-fall if   in the end there is no I   if there
are chrysanthemums afire in blazing beds   if I was the
definition I made when I wore my young self   if   I
was my young self made of mirror & sweetgum &
synthetic   silks because time is a grifter because you
promised & I agreed   because it is Sunday & there is
this ache & even oranges   tea leaves   prayer flags &
demitasse spoons can't make the words   I want   to
say   that   I was a child   every moment I slept against
you & your sheets & the indigo perfume of sunset
always was already inside of the room   we could never
fill with wishes or flowers or children spinning into
their own dizzy graces inside the sweet safety of their
bodies   their youths

Before I Believed in the Body as Word

I went to love because I wanted to believe

in the self as a place that deserved its own
destruction. I dwelled on the inside of my

body as a room & found it lacking light,

dearly undoored, found it stuffed to the rafters
with paper, history, languaged by gun & by

fist. I found inside of my body a suffering

I could justify only through blame & so
I blamed the borders of the body. It was

easy. I dwelled inside of the outside I used

to look for love. By sweetness & saber, I high-
wayed every distance to defeat. I lay down

a bridge into a country trimmed crimson,

split into the only I defined by my own lies.

In the Absence of Desire I Was No Longer Absent

This is the place. I have left
you & every other indecision,

every adverb, every snake of smoke
making its way from London to fog &

listen, I never promised or passioned,
I never pretended to be anything other.

Red-drunk, wine-lipped, I gave you
the best of myself when I gave you the wall

& the wall & the wall. When I roomed
with empty. When I slept with the blonde

sheets in that blank space & under the eyes
of the bachelor-buttoned duvet. We both watched

my hand as it made the light go out & then
we were happy. We had nothing to watch.

We shared our own sweet & separate breathing,
midnight a lulled pulse, all light & its lavendared

inverses. I never slept so well as I did with
that peace. It was beautiful without brutality,

I was beautiful without the steel & hiss of wanting.

House Is a Hoard

House stuffs its walls with mice and men's
magazines. All fall, House hosts an exhibit

of squirrels and their acorns. House has
a hard time letting go. House keeps

its upside-down electric outlets and House
keeps them upside-down. They stare

with their slots of eyes, their small mouths
open always in surprise. House doesn't care

about your intentions, your repairs. House dares
you. House dares you again. House is an artist

of rain and its remnants. Your tarps
and bathtubs are parts of its installation.

House reminds you: your will is only
your will. Your will is not a wall.

The Museum of the Body

First they hang each of your aches
from the eaves. Then the curator comes
with her stickpins, her white cards,

her typeset: *head-, heart-, ear-,*
belly-. The collectors start
small. They take your pinkie toe,

which you miss only at the start of each
startling morning. They come for your skin
in slow pieces. Soon you're accustomed

to muscle, the ruby and the glint of it. Soon
you admire the white hint of bone. The museum
walls fill: a vertebra. Scapula. The pale

plain of ilium, ischium, the pubis
no longer embarrassing without its rough
shock of curls. There is a guide to lead

you from kneecap to talus bone. There
are words, finally. They explain: *see here*
the scar from a second grade bike wreck.

See here the thumb. See the nail asleep
in its bed. You are given headphones.
They tell you: *here is the cranium,*

mandible, the ear and all the words
it drummed. Love and fear. Echo. Here the long
strands of hair you never asked to own.

With All the Certainty of Space

I held a ruler to my feet to find some way
that my steps counted. I knew my fingers
as the space between them. I told myself
to walk. Twenty-six steps to the door, to
the car keys bragging their silvers beside it,
to the odometer clicking off mile & mile until

the oil burned itself out into a measure of
the nothing that we were. I built a tower
to everything I had to know. Siding with brick,
trunked & treed, I climbed. When I lost
the last glimpse of his blue shirt, I became

my own back, my own arms strong
as the act of moving until distance became
the place beyond measure, the peace
of my own motion, stilled.

The Imposition of Ashes

Let the sky break
into bone. I will stand
unshaken in the hollow

of this weather
holding my own
hand upward, lake-

ward. I will empty
the rain. I will refuse
to. I will believe if

a god of my own
making awakens to
thunder into a heaven

that's never a place.
I will believe there are
no directions but if and if

I believe, it is
in the god of
the space between

my body and my self
in sleep, in the ragged black
ash of my own breath.

The Daughter I Will Never Have

                                        has lost all
of her grandmother's diamonds. Has tattooed
onto her left arm the name of the boy

she loved two years before she learned
that to love is to surrender to love but never
to surrender the self. Has learned never to surrender

the self. Has learned to love. Has blonde hair, red
hair, brown hair. Has bleached her eyebrows and then
brown-dyed them back two weeks before her first

college Christmas. Has refused to fly home for her second
college Christmas. Has lost her plane ticket. Has lost
her monthly rent check. Has lost her damn mind. Has broken

my trust before I could earn hers. The daughter I couldn't
have wants a kitten. Wants a pony. Wants a cherry in her drink.
Wants Jeremy to notice her, wants cherry Chapstick,

wants a cherry lollipop, wants to know what Jeremy means
when he says that girls have cherries. Wants me to shut up.
Wants me to sit down, to stand up, wants me to love her,

love her. Wants me to just go away and die. The daughter
I could never have lives in a somewhere far from my everywhere
and inside of my if. And if I imagine her long enough, I can

almost touch the knots that tie themselves into the hair
at the top of her neck. I can almost touch her neck. I can
almost count her ten fingers, her ten toes, I can almost count

up to twenty again and then to her two legs and her two arms,
to the top of her head and the zero that crowns it, the blank
spot I would have cradled and feared before she learned to hold

her head up, before she learned to fear me, to call me mother,
before she even learned to wish or refused to pray. I can almost
touch her shoulder blades and tell her that they are the sharp artifacts

of wings, of a time when we all believed in God as our own
bodies, of a time when we believed that would be enough.

Beneath The Highway, Between Two Nights

Under the shudder of winter I made
my peace with the train, its innuendos
and arrivals, its violent keening
and smoke. When I looked past

the wall I could see where I was
not. I could see against the horizon
a smattering of faces. They had their order
and their number. I was smiling

at a vase. I was happy
as a cardigan. I was always over-
hearing a private chat with
the rain. When I began driving

it was not towards but against
the realization of each mile
I had privileged as much
as the silence that mossed

itself into my lungs. An overhang
of freesia and the dark ecstasy
of forgiveness, which is a needle ticking
upwards, skin to speed to speed.

A Breviary

Instead of saying *early*, the morning strung
its beaded condensation over the clarity

of glass where all of the morning a cat's tongue,
barbed and thirsty, licked a way towards cool.

The window couldn't tell and so it showed: a flock
of leaves, azaleas, asphalt, and what could the woman

who tried to look out do but listen, inside an evening
angled under a sun flushed as any need to leave. The window

repeated, reversed, her own face, holy as blue. What
could she do but hear a thousand petalled words for *faith*

in nothing less than the self that counts all morning
along with every burn and beauty.

The Night Office

Even through winter with all its small hands
I gathered from the clearing its song—
a bouquet of eighth notes, the long

opened O of the whole. This orchestra
of cottonwoods. This swirl of bentgrass. This sky

is a lesson more patient than snow and its weight.
What could my body practice but opening. What
could I do but wonder out towards more light.

Beyond Love

If the saints are to be believed, if this body is a dress
we slip into, out of, if each day and night is the mantle
we tie around our shoulders, fabric thin as the time it takes
teeth to flatten the end of a thread and lead it through

an eyed needle, then what am I to make of the gorgeous
terror every star makes out of its own distance? Sometimes
I can see the body as a blaze, bright-gloried, flamed
and holy as a pin-prick the size of a soul. And if the soul

is a blaze to be believed, then belief blazes a highway
to some beyond, a beauty that begins with every ordinary
sweetness, every one small but still indefinable love.
Every morning, when I wash the wrongs I've made right

out of my hair, I want to believe in each drop of water
as a promise of and from the all that we're meant to contain.

Acknowledgements and Notes

45th Parallel: "The First Time After Surgery" and "The gods have a bullet"

Adanna Literary Journal: "We Decided to Stop Believing in God"

Aesthetica: "Epithalamium"

American Literary Review: "The Museum of the Body"

Amethyst Arsenic: "The Coyote Doesn't Have To"

The Boiler: "The Summer I Wondered Why Dresses Exist"

Cave Wall: "Alma"

Clementine Poetry Journal: "Morphine"

Colorado Review: "Beyond Love"

Compose: "Because the Body Is a Place Strange, Unmapped" and "House Is a Hoard"

Conduit: "House Is an Enigma"

Escape Into Life: "Between Sea and Sky," "I Was a Bad Child & I Was a Match," and "Melancholy Inside Gardens"

Fairy Tale Review: "In Every Tale About Hunger"

Foundry: "Downburst" and "A Breviary"

Handsome Poetry Journal: "Melancholy in Mike Sheroda" and "The Night Office"

Helen: "The Reports of the Largest Moon in Ten Years"

Jabberwock Review: "House Is Writing a Symphony" and "I Am Writing a Story and You Are Reading It"

Josephine Quarterly: "Deposition: On That Night & All That Was After"

IthacaLit: "I Was Told Not To Write About the Body" and "The Daughter I Will Never Have"

interrupture: "Of Flora, Of Fauna"

Mixed Fruit: "Let's Talk About the Weather, That's Probably for the Best."

Muse/A Journal: "Excavation, Exhibition"

The Museum of Americana: "Beneath the Highway, Between Two Nights"

National Poetry Review: "House Is the Word the Doctors Used for My Body"

Nice Cage: "An Unmothered Guide to Grief," "The Plight Troth," and "Shower Season"

New Madrid: "Creation Myth With Language and Angels" and "The Talking Cure"

The Pinch: "The Cities We Love Are The Ones That Are Drowning"

Printer's Devil Review: "That Cold Snap, April's Last"

Quiddity: "The Curse on the Ground" and "Tropes"

The Quotable: "The Study of Surfaces, The Study of Curves"

RHINO: "Of Blue Morning"

Salamander: "Before I Believed in the Body as Word"

Segue: "Because of the House We Have Built for Our Language"

Sinking City: "Under Threat of Eden"

Sliver of Stone: "On the Self-Guided Tour of the Fountain of Youth"

So to Speak: "Describe the Situation in Specific Detail"

Spoon River Poetry Review: "After the Beginning," "For the Doctor Who Suggested I Try to Explain How It Feels to Be Barren," "It was no more predictable," and "My little apparition, my little ghost"

Tinge Magazine: "Melancholy in Definitions" and "That Night In (The Car & The Inside & Outside & So)"

The Tishman Review: "In Ithaca" and "After Auden"

Toad: "Melancholy Inside the Body"

TriQuarterly: "Hysterectomy/Recovery," "The Imposition of Ashes" and "Yes, I Would Like to Imagine the Self"

VOLT: "Having lived beyond"

Waccamaw: "X"

Wherewithal: "Viscera"

"House Is an Enigma" was included in *The Best American Poetry 2015*.

"Of Flora, Of Fauna" was included on the National Endowment for the Arts' 2017 Creative Writing Fellows Writers' Corner.

"It was no more predictable" won the 2014 *Spoon River Poetry Review* Editor's Prize; "My little apparition, my little ghost" was the first runner-up.

"Describe the Situation in Specific Detail" won the 2015 *So to Speak* Feminist Poetry Contest.

"After Auden" was a finalist for *The Tishman Review*'s 2015 Edna St. Vincent Millay Prize.

"X" was reprinted in *Waccamaw: A Journal of Contemporary Literature: A 10-year Retrospective*.

"In Every Tale About Hunger" was a finalist for the 2014 *Fairy Tale Review* poetry contest.

"Let's Talk About the Weather, That's Probably for the Best" was a semi-finalist for the Carson Prize in Poetry from *Mixed Fruit.*

"Pain Serves" incorporates found language—and descriptions of photographs—from "Does Pain Serve a Purpose?" posted on the Did You Know Website: http://www.myuniversalfacts. com/2005/10/does-pain-serve-purpose.html.

"That Cold Snap, April's Last" originated as an exercise from one of my students, and is dedicated to them.

"The Reports of the Largest Moon in Ten Years" is for Gina, J., and my Kentucky crew.

"Melancholy in Mike Sheroda" is dedicated to my friends from Constable Terrace.

"X" includes a quote from Anna Bertha Röntgen, wife of Wilhelm Röntgen, who discovered the x-ray. Upon seeing the first x-ray image ever taken—of her own hand—Anna Bertha Röntgen reportedly said, "I have seen my death!"

Thank you to the friends, family, and readers who supported me through the writing of these poems -- and, well, everything -- especially Chantel Acevedo, Eloisa Amezcua, Julianna Baggott, Aaron Brame, Dustin Brookshire, James Doyle Brown, Pat Byrd, Garrard Conley, Kristin Czarnecki, Phyllis Dallas, Kristina Marie Darling, Hannah Dela Cruz Abrams, Emari DiGiorgio, Danielle DiTiberus, Anthony Frame, Ethan Fulgate, Cory Funk, Christian Anton Gerard, Avery M. Guess, Rachel Hawkins, James Tate Hill, Allison Hull, Kate Knapp Johnson, Sally J. Johnson, Emily Johnston, Nicole Karapanagiotis, Catherine Lawrence, Les Loncharich, M.D. Meyers, Cassie Mannes Murray, Jessica Nastal-Dema, Molly Bess Rector, Ashley Roach-Freiman, Mike Scalise, Kate Scelsa, Bettye Stewart, Emily Van Duyne, Laura von Holt, Brigitte Wallinger-Schorn, Quinn White, Ross White, and Kirstin Hotelling Zona.

All of my love and gratitude to my parents, Cheryl and David Bolden, who opened their home to me, supported me, and saved me.

My love and gratitude to Katie Dobosz-Kenney, who walked through fire with me and kept me safe and sane.

Thank you to Beth, Harriet, Jody, Kim Waldrup, Little Rue, Marty, and Team Seven.

Thank you to my FAV family.

To Susan Swartwout for choosing this book and to James Brubaker and everyone at Southeast Missouri State University Press – thank you, a hundred times, for giving *House* a home.

My deepest gratitude to the National Endowment for the Arts, whose generous grant supported the writing of these poems.